IMAGES
of America
CLARK COUNTY

NEVADA STATE MUSEUM, LAS VEGAS. The Nevada State Museum, Las Vegas is one of seven managed by the state Division of Museums and History, an agency of the Nevada Department of Cultural Affairs. The department serves Nevada's citizens and visitors through cultural and information management, presentation and promotion of cultural resources, and education. The department also includes the State Office of Historic Preservation, Nevada State Library and Archives, and the Nevada Arts Council.

ON THE COVER: A solitary figure at the Kiel Ranch in the early 1900s pauses by a small spring in what is now North Las Vegas. Early settlers in Clark County relied on water from springs and artesian wells. (Courtesy of Nevada State Museum, Las Vegas.)

Crystal R. Van Dee
Nevada State Museum, Las Vegas

ISBN 978-1-5316-4563-2

Published by Arcadia Publishing
Charleston, South Carolina

Library of Congress Control Number: 2008940180

For all general information contact Arcadia Publishing at:
Telephone 843-853-2070
Fax 843-853-0044
E-mail sales@arcadiapublishing.com
For customer service and orders:
Toll-Free 1-888-313-2665

Visit us on the Internet at www.arcadiapublishing.com

I dedicate this book to my beautiful mom, Rose Marie Van Dee; Jeff Dugan, my amazingly patient and loving husband; and finally, Anthony Minielli, my brother.

Contents

ACKNOWLEDGMENTS

Many people helped me with this book, and I owe them a great deal of gratitude and love. Thank you to Dennis McBride for suggesting that I take on this book. Thank you to Debbie Seracini, my Arcadia editor, who encouraged me with her pep talks. I would also like to thank Jeff Dugan, Paul Carson, and David Millman for help with research and captions.

All photographs used in this book are from the Nevada State Museum, Las Vegas, unless otherwise noted.

Introduction

In 1905, when Las Vegas was born, Clark County did not exist. Las Vegas, along with Searchlight, El Dorado Canyon, Goodsprings, Bunkerville, and several other areas were part of Lincoln County. Pioche, the county seat, was over 200 miles away from Las Vegas, a distance prohibitive to conducting business. No railroads connected the area, and the trip by horse took days. Not only was the trip time consuming, it was expensive and sometimes dangerous because of the desert terrain. In some cases, it was easier to take care of matters in Kingman, Arizona. This was especially true for miners registering their claims.

Political and economic pressure from prominent southern Nevadans eventually led to the 1909 creation of Clark County. Although Searchlight was booming in the early 20th century, the presence of the San Pedro, Los Angeles, and Salt Lake Railroad proved a deciding factor in choosing Las Vegas as the county seat.

The railroad was instrumental to the success of Clark County, especially Las Vegas. The county's connection to the railroad became painfully clear when Union Pacific, the new owner of the San Pedro, Los Angeles, and Salt Lake Railroad, moved the repair yards from Las Vegas to Caliente in Lincoln County in 1922 in response to a labor strike. Although Las Vegas still maintained the train depot, the loss of the repair yards meant that many workers were suddenly unemployed. Searchlight also faced economic troubles as the mine profits gradually diminished. Although mines in El Dorado Canyon and Nelson remained profitable until the 1940s, other mines in areas like Goodsprings suffered the same fate as Searchlight.

An economic boost came in the late 1920s in the form of federal government legislation that led to the creation of Hoover Dam. Clark County's long border with Arizona helped ensure that nearby Nevada towns would benefit from the construction of the dam. A housing area developed near the planned dam site, and a new town, Boulder City, was created. Dam workers traveled to Las Vegas for entertainment, and the city's economy shifted from the remnants of the railroad to gambling and tourism. It is also during this time that Las Vegas officials began marketing the town as a primary destination for quick and easy divorces and marriages.

Boulder City was a microcosm of the United States because it housed dam workers from all over the country. City planners intended that Boulder City be abandoned after the completion of the dam. However, after working on the dam for several years, many workers and their families remained in the area, and Boulder City continued to grow.

In the intervening years between the completion of the dam and World War II, Clark County residents enjoyed the new culture that developed from their diverse backgrounds. Las Vegas celebrated the annual Helldorado Days, an imaginative retelling of the town's history. Civilian Conservation Corps workers helped create roads through Mount Charleston and assisted in the excavation of Lost City, the ruins of a Native American settlement near Overton. Clark County's population grew at a steady rate.

As the uses of magnesium became militarily important for U.S. allies in the late 1930s and early 1940s, new plants were essential and Basic Magnesium Incorporated (BMI) began a large plant just outside of Las Vegas. Similar to the employment boom of the Hoover Dam, workers from all over the United States immigrated to the area. Their town site, Basic, eventually became Henderson. For the first time, African Americans came to Clark County in large numbers as BMI employees. Although geographically close to Las Vegas, Henderson created its own identity, complete with separate libraries, churches, and schools.

By this time, Las Vegas's famous casino industry was well underway. Las Vegas casinos had been popular since the 1930s, but it wasn't until the construction of El Rancho Vegas in 1941 that Las Vegas became a resort town. Other casinos quickly followed, including the Flamingo in 1946 and Desert Inn in 1950.

Las Vegas resorts have dominated the public perception of Clark County, but that is only part of the county's history. From mining operations to mega-resorts, Clark County has existed under many guises in its 100 years of history. In addition to casino moguls and the federal government, community members and their organizations have contributed to the ever-changing culture and history of Clark County. This book is a photographic celebration of the unique, diverse, and little-known aspects of the county's history.

One

Railroads, Ranches, and Mines

Las Vegas Ranch, 1905. The Las Vegas Ranch was the center of activity for much of the early years of Las Vegas. O. D. Gass owned the ranch between the 1860s and 1870s, but when he ran into financial difficulties, he lost the ranch to Pioche businessman Archibald Stewart. In 1882, Stewart moved his pregnant wife, Helen, and their three children, William, Hiram, and Eliza, to Las Vegas.

Helen Stewart, Late 1800s. With the ranch as an important supply source for many coming through the area, Helen Stewart was always busy. She was still settling into life on the ranch, and pregnant with Archie Jr., when her husband was murdered at Kiel Ranch in 1884. Instead of doing the expected and moving away, Helen remained in Las Vegas and helped turn it into a boomtown.

Mesquite Club, 1910s. The Mesquite Club is the oldest women's organization in Las Vegas. Helen Stewart (center) was one of the founding members of the club. It was her idea to name the club after the hardy mesquite tree. Here the women are in costume for a special event.

THREE GENERATIONS OF STEWARTS, 1910s. Helen Stewart, her daughter Eva Stewart Stay, and grandson Clarence Archie Stay Jr. pose in Helen's garden. Helen was very protective of her children, and while they were away, she wrote to them on an almost weekly basis. Helen was especially fond of her youngest son, Archie Jr., and when he died in a riding accident, she was devastated.

HELEN STEWART IN GARDEN, 1924. Helen Stewart was an avid reader and writer. She was considered a historian and was the first postmaster of Las Vegas. She also wrote poetry that she shared with her family. She has been called "First Lady of Las Vegas," in part because it was her land that the railroad purchased and auctioned off as Clark's Las Vegas town site in 1905. She died in 1926.

Campers on Las Vegas Creek, Early 1900s. Many families moved to Las Vegas without precise plans for living quarters. Some families, like the one in this photograph, set up their belongings

Building on Las Vegas Ranch, around 1904. This building was located somewhere on the Las Vegas Ranch and served as the first store, hotel, and post office for the growing town. Helen Stewart, owner of the ranch, served as the town's first postmaster. In writing to her daughter Eliza "Tiza," Stewart always reminded her to append the address with Lincoln or Clark County, Nevada, so that the mail would not be delivered to Las Vegas, New Mexico.

in makeshift camps as they waited for their homes to be built. The tent structure to the left was set up as a bathhouse.

Hotel Las Vegas, 1905. Most of the hotels in early Las Vegas began as tents with raised floors. When William Clark's railroad auctioned the land that became the town of Las Vegas, many visitors stayed in rustic hotels like the one shown here.

Las Vegas Creek, 1909. Joe and Frances Farnsworth pose for a playful photograph at Las Vegas Creek. The water sources scattered throughout Clark County have attracted people for thousands of years. The first people to use the springs were Native Americans. European explorers and traders followed, first the Spanish in the 18th century and then traders using the Spanish Trail. In the mid-19th century, John C. Frémont led several government-sponsored expeditions to map the American West. During his stop in what was to become Las Vegas, he said that the water was palatable but too warm to drink at 71 degrees.

RAILROAD DEPOT, 1905. When the San Pedro, Los Angeles, and Salt Lake Railroad first came to Las Vegas, this railcar served as a multiuse depot. It was the passenger waiting room, ticket booth, and the office for Pacific Fruit Express. It was also the office for the Western Union telegraph office.

LAS VEGAS, 1905. This photograph was taken from the vantage point of the San Pedro, Los Angeles, and Salt Lake Railroad depot, which was still under construction in August 1905.

1913

Las Vegas, Nevada

Where Farming Pays

EGLINGTON WELL, NEAR LAS VEGAS
OVER 600 GALLONS OF WATER PER MINUTE

The Artesian Belt of Semi-Tropic Nevada

Issued by the
CHAMBER OF COMMERCE
LAS VEGAS, NEVADA

LAS VEGAS BROCHURE, 1913. This brochure was geared toward farmers and enticed them to move to Las Vegas with the promise that Clark County was the "artesian belt of Semi-Tropic Nevada." The Las Vegas Chamber of Commerce wrote the brochure, hoping readers would not realize that most of Clark County was an arid desert. Artesian wells were common in Las Vegas, but in many cases, water resources were poorly managed. For example, the uncapped well in this brochure was reported to produce 600 gallons of water every minute. Over time, the water table has lowered, while the population of Clark County has grown to over two million.

SAN PEDRO, LOS ANGELES, AND SALT LAKE RAILROAD DEPOT, 1906. Construction on this mission-style building began in 1905 and was completed in 1906. Positioned at the west end of Fremont Street, the depot serviced this area until 1940 when it was torn down in favor of a more modern building. A similar depot remains standing about two hours southwest of Las Vegas in Kelso, California.

LOS ANGELES LIMITED

A PALATIAL TRAIN FOR PARTICULAR PEOPLE

RUNS DAILY SOLID

BETWEEN **CHICAGO and LOS ANGELES** VIA

SALT LAKE ROUTE, UNION PACIFIC R. R. CHICAGO & NORTHWESTERN RY.

TO LOS ANGELES

	STATIONS	Time	DAYS OF THE WEEK
Lv	CHICAGO	10.05PM	Mon. Tues. Wed. Thurs. Fri. Sat. Sun
Lv	CEDAR RAPIDS	3.40AM	Tues. Wed. Thurs. Fri. Sat. Sun. Mon
Lv	OMAHA	12.06PM	" " " " " " "
Lv	CHEYENNE	1.05AM	Wed. Thurs. Fri. Sat. Sun. Mon. Tues
Lv	OGDEN	5.20PM	" " " " " " "
Ar	SALT LAKE CITY	6.25PM	" " " " " " "
Lv	SALT LAKE CITY	6.45PM	" " " " " " "
Lv	CALIENTE	6.00AM	Thurs. Fri. Sat. Sun. Mon. Tues. Wed.
Lv	LAS VEGAS	8.50AM	" " " " " " "
Lv	DAGGETT	2.00PM	" " " " " " "
Lv	SAN BERNARDINO	5.05PM	" " " " " " "
Lv	RIVERSIDE	5.40PM	" " " " " " "
Lv	POMONA	6.20PM	" " " " " " "
Ar	LOS ANGELES	7.15PM	" " " " " " "
Ar	PASADENA	8.05PM	Thurs. Fri. Sat. Sun. Mon. Tues. Wed.

TO CHICAGO

	STATIONS	Time	DAYS OF THE WEEK
	PASADENA	1.55PM	Mon. Tues. Wed. Thurs. Fri. Sat. Sun.
Lv	LOS ANGELES	2.45PM	" " " " " " "
Lv	POMONA	3.31PM	" " " " " " "
Lv	RIVERSIDE	4.12PM	" " " " " " "
Lv	SAN BERNARDINO	5.00PM	" " " " " " "
Lv	DAGGETT	7.55PM	" " " " " " "
Lv	LAS VEGAS	2.20AM	Tues. Wed. Thurs. Fri. Sat. Sun. Mon.
Lv	CALIENTE	6.25AM	" " " " " " "
Ar	SALT LAKE CITY	5.35PM	" " " " " " "
Lv	SALT LAKE CITY	5.55PM	" " " " " " "
Lv	OGDEN	7.00PM	" " " " " " "
Lv	CHEYENNE	9.40AM	Wed. Thurs. Fri. Sat. Sun. Mon. Tues.
Lv	OMAHA	11.00PM	" " " " " " "
Ar	CEDAR RAPIDS	6.00AM	Thurs. Fri. Sat. Sun. Mon. Tues. Wed.
Ar	CHICAGO	11.55AM	" " " " " " "

DIRECT CONNECTION IS MADE AT LOS ANGELES WITH PARLOR CARS TO AND FROM PASADENA. BAGGAGE MAY BE CHECKED THROUGH TO AND FROM ALL POINTS.

"The LOS ANGELES LIMITED" A solid vestibuled train operated daily between Los Angeles and Chicago without change. The equipment consists of Pullman Standard Drawing Room and Private Compartment and Tourist sleeping cars, Observation—Library—Buffet Cars, and Dining Cars, all electrically lighted throughout. A library is furnished for the accommodation of passengers, and each berth in the Standard Sleepers provided with separate reading lights.

"The OVERLAND" Operated daily between Los Angeles and Salt Lake City, equipped with Chair Cars (seats free), coaches, Standard and Tourist Sleepers and Dining Cars. This train carries Standard Sleepers in connection with the D. & R. G. R. R. to and from Denver without change. Also Tourist Sleepers as follows:

Via Union Pacific R. R. and C. & N. W. Ry. to and from Omaha and Chicago.
Via D. & R. G. R. R. and Burlington Route to and from Omaha and Chicago.
Via D. & R. G. R. R. and Missouri Pacific Railway to and from Kansas City and St. Louis, (semi-weekly).
Via D. & R. G., U. P. and Northwestern line to and from Denver, Omaha, St. Paul and Minneapolis, (Weekly).

The DINING CAR SERVICE on both the "Los Angeles Limited" and the "Overland" is conceded to have no superior in the West. Through cars are attached to all trains, thereby doing away with the objectionable hasty meal at wayside lunch counters. All meals a la carte.

Times-Mirror P. & B. House, L. A. April '07—52,000

RAILROAD SCHEDULE, 1907. The San Pedro, Los Angeles, and Salt Lake Railroad offered trips from Las Vegas to Los Angeles or Salt Lake City every day of the week. The train bound for Los Angeles left at 8:50 in the morning.

Freight Team, 1905. Once materials were transported to Las Vegas via train, they still had to make the trip to the outlying mining districts throughout southern Nevada. Freight teams were a common sight in the new town. The wagons were capable of such extraordinary loads that 14-horse teams were required to haul the cargo.

Block and Botkins Gent's Furnishings, 1905. Located on Fremont Street between First and Second Streets, Block and Botkins was one of the few places in Clark County where men could purchase clothing, hats, and shoes. Even in the heat of Clark County, men and women wore full-length clothing.

Las Vegas Street Scene, 1910. Las Vegas was founded in 1905, but it wasn't until 1909 that Clark County was created, with Las Vegas as the county seat. Before the creation of Clark County, residents in the southernmost portions of the state had to travel 200 miles to Pioche to conduct county business.

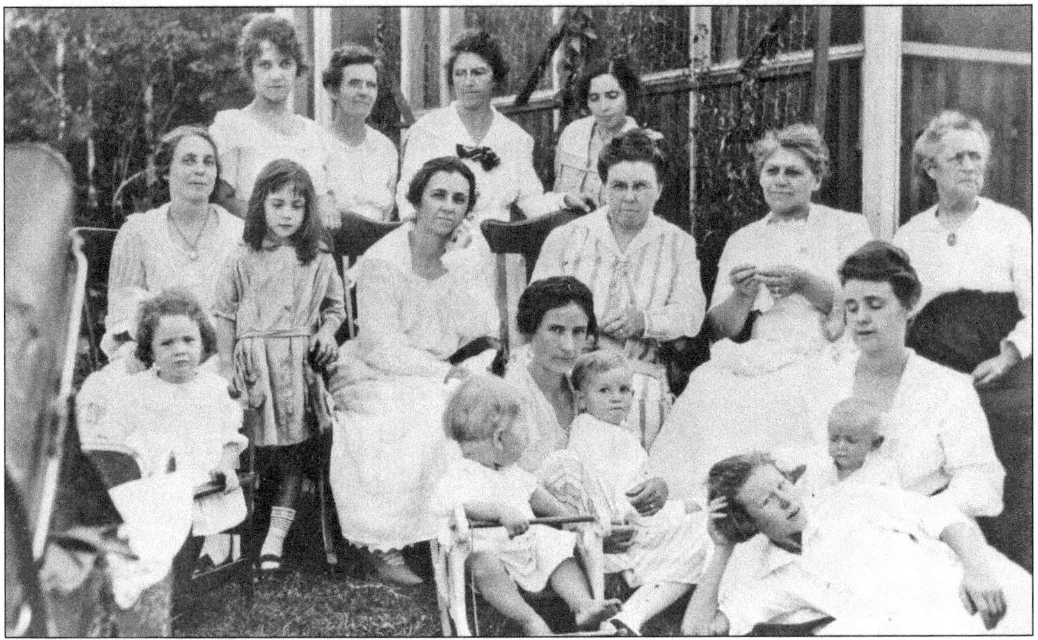

Las Vegas Hostess Club, 1910s. The Las Vegas Hostess Club was created early in the town's history. Women hosted meetings where members could sew, chat, exchange recipes, and organize charitable work. Children, particularly daughters, also had the opportunity to learn from their mothers. Joining the club was a good way for newcomers to adjust to life in Clark County.

Picnic at Kiel Ranch, 1910s. Kiel Ranch was located several miles from the Las Vegas Ranch. Originally owned by Conrad Kiel, John S. Park bought the ranch when he moved to Las Vegas in the early 1900s. Park built a home on the ranch, as did his son, Dr. William Park. In the late 1800s, Kiel Ranch was the sight of an infamous scene in which Helen Stewart's husband, Archibald Stewart, was murdered under suspicious circumstances. In this photograph, a group of local children enjoys a picnic at the Kiel Ranch home of Dr. Park.

Child at Kiel Ranch, 1910s. A child at Kiel Ranch enjoys a slice of melon during a picnic. Kiel Ranch was irrigated through a series of springs and man-made ditches. Located in what is now North Las Vegas, the Kiel Ranch provided fresh produce for Las Vegas and the surrounding area. The City of North Las Vegas now owns the remnants of the Kiel Ranch.

Home of John Park, 1910s. John S. Park, who opened and managed the First State Bank in Las Vegas, built this large house on South Fremont Street. The Park family was one of the first to settle in Las Vegas and became involved in many community organizations.

Family in Front of House, Undated. A family stands proudly in front of their home, while a young girl looks down the street. Craftsman-style houses were very popular in early Las Vegas. They were attractive yet affordable homes for the growing middle class. These types of houses once dotted the Las Vegas Valley, but very few still exist.

First State Bank, 1905. Charles "Pop" Squires, J. Ross Clark, and their colleagues began the First State Bank in Las Vegas. With Californian John S. Park managing the operation, the bank was an immediate success. Its existence was influential in establishing Las Vegas as the Clark County seat in 1909. The bank's first home was inside a store, but it was later moved to Second and Fremont Streets.

Delivery Truck, 1910. Although Las Vegas was primarily a railroad town, it reportedly received its first delivery via automobile in 1910 by the truck on the right. The truck on the left is from Troy Laundry. Although automobiles were sometimes convenient, they were often more hindrance than help on the unpaved roads of early Clark County. Horses were more reliable.

Main Street, 1914. Tree-lined streets in Las Vegas were a familiar sight because of the availability of water from springs. The *Las Vegas Age* newspaper periodically recommended that planting trees would beautify the town. The Mesquite Club (see page 10) agreed and made it one of their many projects.

EARLY DOWNTOWN LAS VEGAS, C. 1907. In this photograph, the streets of downtown Las Vegas have yet to be paved. First Street is in the foreground, and it is intersected by Fremont Street. Las Vegas Coffee Shop is across the street from the Tailor Shop. By 1909, the town had 10 miles of graded streets, an opera house, an ice plant, and a telephone exchange.

LADD'S SWIMMING POOL, LATE 1910S OR EARLY 1920S. This swimming pool was opened by Capt. James Ladd in 1911. Located off east Fremont Street, Ladd's resort was a popular place for both locals and tourists. In the water is Art Lewis, and from left to right are (seated) Leslie Lewis, Alta Ham, and Dorothy Lewis; (standing) Artemus Ham, Leo McNamee, Frances McNamee, and Capt. James Ladd.

Peach Orchard, 1921. This local peach orchard was planted in 1917. Irrigation ditches, springs, and wells were important for early farmers in Clark County. In 1909, the same year Clark County was created, the Lincoln County Experimental Farm published detailed advice on how to plan and plant an orchard in a December issue of the *Las Vegas Age*. Ditch irrigation was required for optimal results, and in order to have a pleasing orchard of mixed fruits, the recommended distance between trees was 24 feet.

LEONARD AND GEORGE FAYLE, 1910. Goodsprings is approximately 35 miles southwest of Las Vegas. Seen in this photograph is the Fayle family, one of the most prominent families in Goodsprings. In 1916, in addition to building the Goodsprings Hotel, George Fayle also built a saloon, café, and a general store in the mining town. The Pioneer Saloon is still in operation and remains a popular attraction.

STUDENTS AT GOODSPRINGS, 1928. The students from the fourth- through eighth-grade classes pose near the school. The Goodsprings school house started as a tent in 1907, and a permanent one-room building was finished in 1913, making it the oldest active school building in Clark County. When the school was built, school districts in Clark County were based on cities or townships; now they are organized on the county level.

Goodsprings Hotel, Late 1910s. Built in 1916 by entrepreneur George Fayle, the Goodsprings Hotel offered many amenities in its 20 rooms, including electricity, steam heat, and running water. Las Vegans often made the trip just to enjoy the hotel, also known as the Fayle Hotel. It had some of the best food in Clark County and was very popular in the 1910s and 1920s. Much of the food cooked at the Goodsprings Hotel was purchased from Clark County farms and ranches, like the Tomiyasu Ranch in Las Vegas. Fire destroyed the hotel in 1966.

Women at Goodsprings, 1920s. Women drivers were uncommon. Here two women pause for a break at Goodsprings. In her letters, Helen Stewart frequently commented on the loudness of cars as they passed her home in Las Vegas.

Potosi Mine, 1917. Mark Sullivan and Merle Sheppard pose near the Potosi Mine in the Goodsprings Mining District. Goodsprings area mines were active in the 1910s and experienced a small boom during World War I in response to the demand for wartime materials. Another small boom followed during World War II, but production gradually decreased, and there are very few active mines in the area.

ELDORADO CANYON QUARTZ MILL, 1890S. Eldorado Canyon was a profitable mining area approximately 50 miles south of Las Vegas. Gold, silver, copper, and quartz were the primary materials mined in the area. The Southwest Mining Company owned the quartz mill in this photograph along the Colorado River in Eldorado Canyon. The company was established in 1879, and within 20 years, it owned most of the producing mines in El Dorado Canyon. Southwest Mining Company used its own riverboats to transport ore and other materials along the river.

Home of Mills Family, Early 1900s. In 1884 or 1885, W. S. Mills became the superintendent for the Southwest Mining Company. Shown here is the Mills family home along the Colorado River in Eldorado Canyon. Although in many respects Eldorado Canyon was a frontier mining town, Mills and his family enjoyed a comfortable home because of his position as superintendent. In the bottom photograph, Mount Davis is visible through the open door. Despite the proximity of the Colorado, placer mining at Eldorado Canyon did not yield many results.

Bedroom in the Mills Home, Early 1900s. Found in an old photo album, this photograph is labeled "Lyra's bedroom." Furniture and other household supplies were delivered by steamboat along the Colorado River and by overland freight. Shipping prices were high and would have been cost prohibitive for most of the mine laborers at Eldorado Canyon.

Eldorado Canyon, 1915. Prominent members of Clark County society rest near Eldorado Canyon after a drive. According to the photograph's label, in front of the car on the left is Las Vegas dentist William S. Park and his wife, Mary Belle Viley Park. To the right are David Farnsworth, Isabelle Cunningham, unidentified, and E. M. Simm.

RUINS OF FORT CALLVILLE, 1920S. With hopes of using the Colorado River as a means for transportation of supplies and people, Mormon leader Brigham Young sent Bishop Anson Call to set up an outpost on the river. Founded in the mid-19th century, the post proved very desolate and it was difficult to convince people to stay. In the 1920s, all that remained of the settlement were ruins, now submerged by the waters of Lake Mead.

OVERTON, 1910S. Jack and Jane Connelly and their children pose in front of their Overton home. In 1907, the *Las Vegas Age* described Overton, located 65 miles northwest of Las Vegas, as the "metropolis of Muddy Valley" even though the population was estimated to be only 150. Muddy Valley is sometimes referred to as Moapa Valley, taken from a Paiute word that roughly translates to "muddy water."

LOGANDALE RODEO, 1922. Logandale was first named St. Joseph, was then briefly known as Logan, and then became Logandale. Logandale had a small but thriving ranch community, as seen in the above photograph of a local rodeo. C. L. Averett is seen holding down the horse, while Charles Walsh (center) and Henry Rice (right) look on. Logandale has been the home of the Clark County Fair and Rodeo since the 1960s. Irrigated by the Muddy River, the cornfield pictured below was in Logandale, adjacent to Overton. Located on the Averett Ranch, corn crops such as these provided food for both animals and humans. In front of the field are Ashley Rice and Matt Reese.

Cantaloupe Packing Shed, 1925. Melons, particularly cantaloupes, were one of the primary crops grown in Clark County. This packing shed was located in Logandale near the Averett Ranch. Logandale farmers fought a constant battle with floods. In 1915, a spring flood wiped out 30 acres of grain and damaged soil that had been prepared for cantaloupe seeds.

Train at Apex, 1920s. About 20 miles north of Las Vegas, Apex was a stop on the San Pedro, Los Angeles, and Salt Lake Railroad. It is currently home to a large landfill that services all of Clark County. It is also the starting point for Las Vegas Boulevard. The train tracks at Apex are still used by Union Pacific.

Man at Springs, 1920s. An unidentified man collects water in a marshy area west of Las Vegas. Named by the Spanish-speaking traders, the first European explorers to mention the area, Las Vegas means "the meadows." It refers to the marsh-like growth around local springs. Archaeological evidence of Native Americans has been found near many of Clark County's natural springs. Water was available but scarce, despite claims of Clark County boosters. A 1915 advertisement from the Fidelity Trust Company, hoping to convince people to move to Clark County, proclaimed, "no drouth [*sic*]! No uncertainty in crops! Climate ideal!" Such advertisements are reminiscent of the 19th-century image of the American West as a land of plenty.

First Methodist Episcopal Church, 1920s. The congregation of the First Methodist Episcopal Church is the oldest in Las Vegas, with some of its first services held in tents and private residences. The church building in this image was completed in 1908 but destroyed in a 1922 fire. Volunteer firefighters were quick to arrive, but insufficient water pressure hindered their efforts to save the church. Following the fire, services were held in the grammar school and stores. Church members successfully raised enough funds to build a new church on the site of the old one.

Girl Scouts, 1920s. The Girl Scouts were, and continue to be, an active community organization in Clark County. The unidentified young women in this photograph are enjoying a trip to Mount Charleston with their troop leaders. Like their national counterparts, Girl Scouts in Clark County studied a variety of subjects, including first aid and outdoor skills.

High School Anniversary, 1927. The Clark County High School was built in 1917, and the students in this photograph celebrated the school's 10-year anniversary by dressing in clothes from the previous decade. The school's name was later changed to Las Vegas High School, and a new building was constructed in 1930 to meet the area's growing population.

FREMONT STREET, 1929. Fremont Street was the first paved street in Las Vegas and was a main throughway for automobiles, horses, and pedestrians. Although the street is spelled with an "e" instead of an "é," Fremont Street was named after explorer and politician John C. Frémont. The street was home to businesses as well as many Las Vegas pioneers. This photograph is facing the train depot at the west end of Fremont Street. Arching over the street is a sign that reads, "Welcome to Las Vegas." By 1930, southern Nevada started to see signs of the Depression and anxiously waited for construction to begin on the new dam in Black Canyon near present-day Boulder City.

Two

From Hoover Dam to Helldorado

Dam Location, 1930. By the mid-1920s, Clark County's boom phase appeared to be at an end. In 1922, the railroad moved its repair yards up the line to Caliente in Lincoln County, a move that ended many Clark County jobs. Hope came, however, in the form of a government contract to build a new dam in southern Nevada. Here government agents are scouting the location of the future dam along the Colorado River. Original plans for the dam had it located in Boulder Canyon, but upon further inspection, Black Canyon was chosen as a more appropriate location. The name Boulder, however, had already been attached to the project and people's imaginations.

Employment Line, Early 1930s. Even with the demand for workers on the Hoover Dam, there were simply not enough jobs to meet the needs of Clark County workers. As they were elsewhere in the United States, unemployment levels were high in southern Nevada. Here hundreds of men line up in front of the state employment office with hopes of working on the Hoover Dam.

Arizona Club, 1930s. Las Vegas was famous for "Block 16," an area in downtown reserved for activities like prostitution and bootlegging. Although Las Vegans wanted their town to house the dam workers, the government worried about their safety. The Arizona Club, seen here with prostitutes sitting in the shade, was one of the oldest and most infamous establishments on Block 16.

Las Vegas Rail Depot, 1930s. As people poured into Clark County to work on the dam, the rail depot was once again a center of activity after slowing down in the mid-1920s. Because of the ease of rail travel between Los Angeles, Las Vegas, and Salt Lake City, many people were able to maintain strong connections to these towns.

Sal Sagev Hotel, 1930s. The building in this photograph was originally the Nevada Hotel. When gambling was legalized in 1931, owners changed the name to Sal Sagev (Las Vegas spelled backward) and offered gambling in addition to hotel accommodations. In the 1950s, the Sal Sagev rented space to the Golden Gate Hotel, which eventually bought out the Sal Sagev and took over the rest of the building.

MacDonald Hotel, Early 1930s. Located on Fifth Street, the MacDonald Hotel opened in 1929. The hotel had 39 rooms, 25 of them with private baths. With the impending construction of Hoover Dam, hotel rooms helped relieve the growing housing problem in Clark County. Despite the moneymaking efforts of hotels like the MacDonald, many workers were still left without shelter.

National Hotel, Early 1930s. Las Vegas and Clark County grew quickly in the 1930s because of the Hoover Dam project. In 1929, the National Hotel was one of several in Las Vegas that benefitted from a new "pay-station" telephone system created in response to growing consumer demand.

ENTRANCE TO BOULDER CITY, 1930S. Concerned with gambling and Las Vegas's apparently casual attitudes about Prohibition, the government opted to create the reservation of Boulder City rather than house workers in Las Vegas. U.S. deputy marshall George P. Roy stopped every car that entered Boulder City to insure its occupants had official business on the reservation.

EDITH POWELL, 1930S. People hopeful for work moved their families to southern Nevada despite an alarming housing shortage. Many people lived in a tent town near the site of the dam project while they waited for their homes to be built in Boulder City. Edith Powell, the wife of a dam contractor, was the first woman to live in the town.

Anderson Mess Hall, 1931. It took a small army to feed the dam workers. In this photograph, employees from the Anderson Mess Hall are dressed in their characteristic white uniforms. The mess hall was massive, and the men ate in shifts. Workers expended a great deal of energy during the shifts, and it was up to the mess hall to see that they were properly nourished.

Mess Hall Food, 1930s. In this publicity shot, a dam worker illustrates the plentiful food provided by the mess hall. In a menu from 1932, workers were offered a wide array of food from veal to fried eggplant. The men could eat all they liked, but they had to eat everything they took so that nothing would go to waste.

Diversion Tunnel, 1931. Before Hoover Dam could be built, the water of the Colorado had to be diverted. This was accomplished in part by the construction of several diversion tunnels. Once the tunnels were clear of debris, they were lined with concrete. Despite the dangerous and daunting task, workers finished the tunnels a year ahead of schedule.

Dam Construction, 1930s. During the height of its construction, Hoover Dam, once known as Boulder Dam, employed approximately 5,000 people. This number does not include the support personnel who were essential to the project. For 24 hours a day, 7 days a week, with pauses only for the Fourth of July and Christmas, laborers worked continuously from 1931 to 1936.

Boulder City, around 1934. Six Companies, the contractor for Hoover Dam, built employee housing seven miles from the construction site. The resulting town was named Boulder City. The demand for houses was so great that families could spend up to two years waiting for a home. Boulder City was federally managed until 1958.

Lost City, 1930s. Although Lake Mead created a new recreation area, it also submerged towns, mines, and archaeological sites. Lost City, the ruins of a Puebloan village, was one of the areas covered by Lake Mead. National Park Service archaeologists rushed to excavate and catalog their discoveries, taking only several years on a project that would normally take decades. Artifacts from the site were eventually housed in the Lost City Museum in Overton.

St. Thomas Envelope, 1938. St. Thomas was another Clark County treasure lost to the waters of Lake Mead. When the waters of Lake Mead are low, the ruins of St. Thomas are sometimes visible. Because of this, the town is under the watchful eye of the National Park Service. This envelope, showing buildings in a growing lake, is the last day cover for the small town.

EMERY FALLS, 1937. Murl Emery was a Colorado River boatman who offered his services before, during, and after the construction of Hoover Dam. When families first moved into the area and lived in tent cities, Emery and his family helped provide them with supplies. Here his boat is seen near Emery Falls shortly after the creation of Lake Mead.

B. J. Stevenson, 1939. Parked on South Second Street in Las Vegas, longtime resident B. J. Stevenson shows off a 1929 Durant.

Boulder Club, 1935. Located on 118 East Fremont Street, the Boulder Club opened in 1929 in anticipation of the upcoming Boulder Dam Project. The club was furnished with a hardwood bar, officially used to serve soft drinks but in reality used to serve illegal liquor. The club offered gambling as well, which was also illegal until 1931.

The

Boulder Club

A Gentleman's Resort

SOFT DRINKS . . . CIGARS
CIGARETTES . . . TOBACCOS

Telephone 335 | 118 FREMONT ST. | Las Vegas, Nevada

[42]

Boulder Club Advertisement, 1930s. In this advertisement from an unknown magazine, the Boulder Club is marketed as a Gentlemen's Club. Boulder Club owners sought to elevate the establishment above the image of a common saloon and decorated the interior with luxurious materials. The outside was graced with a 12-foot-tall neon sign.

Fourth/Fifth Street School, 1934. Located at Fourth and Fifth Streets and intersected by Clark Street, this school held classes for grades five through eight. The 1934 fire shown in this photograph destroyed the school's largest building. Luckily, classes had already been dismissed and no one was harmed. Students were not granted a day of rest or mourning for their school. Classes resumed in the high school gym the next morning.

Las Vegas High School, 1940s. Designed to hold 500 students, the Las Vegas High School opened in 1930 under the guidance of Las Vegas School superintendent Maude Frazier. Residents scoffed at building such a large school and complained that its location on Seventh Street and Bridger Street was too far away.

Fire Truck, Undated. The REO factory sent this photograph of the new Las Vegas Fire Department fire truck once the truck was ready for shipment. The truck in this photograph is an REO Speedwagon. It was one of the trucks to respond to the Fourth/Fifth Street School fire in 1934, but the truck broke down and an older truck, a Model T, was used instead.

Volunteer Fire Department, 1930s. The Las Vegas Volunteer Fire Department began in 1906, shortly after the creation of the town. The fire department was staffed completely by volunteers until 1942. Residents lovingly called members of the department "fire boys," and in 1924, a local journalist wrote that the men deserved community support because "they have fought the fire demon for us."

Las Vegas Hospital, 1931. In the 1930s, many businesses and homes were still centered in the Fremont Street area. The same was true for the Las Vegas Hospital, seen in this photograph. Built in 1931 on Eighth Street and Ogden Street, this hospital replaced the original hospital operating out of the former Palace Hotel on Second Street.

Roy Martin, 1930. The hospital's first doctor was Roy Martin, a longtime physician in the area who once worked as a surgeon for the San Pedro, Los Angeles, and Salt Lake Railroad. Martin and his colleagues were responsible for creating the first hospital in the old Palace Hotel, the 1931 hospital on Ogden, and a hospital in Goodsprings.

Union Pacific Baseball Team, 1930s. Purchased by the Union Pacific in 1922, the railroad remained an important part of Southern Nevadans' lives. The new owners almost immediately started a baseball team made up of Union Pacific employees.

Lorenzi Resort Pool, 1933. Opened in the mid-1920s, Lorenzi Resort in Las Vegas was a popular recreation spot in Clark County, especially during the summer. The owner and creator, David Lorenzi, built two lakes and filled them with water from a well on the site of the resort. Later he built a swimming pool graced with a tall fountain (see pages 103–104).

Wimpy's Restaurant, 1935. Wimpy's opened in 1933 and was located at 210 East Fremont Street in Las Vegas. The restaurant, inspired by a character in *Popeye*, served "good home cooked foods at reasonable prices," including Wimpy's Hamburgers. The octagonal-shaped restaurant featured a brightly colored "spic & span" interior and drive-up service.

LAS VEGAS LAUNDRY COMPANY, 1939. The Las Vegas Laundry Company targeted housewives when they told women to "stop drowning in a tubful of work." Located at 701 South First Street, the company offered pick-up and delivery service and charged 5¢ for each pound of laundry.

MOUNT CHARLESTON, 1940S. Long used as a source for lumber, Mount Charleston eventually became a resort area for Clark County residents seeking relief from the desert heat. At nearly 12,000 feet, Mount Charleston has much cooler temperatures than the rest of Clark County. Surrounded by desert, Mount Charleston sits alone like an island and has many indigenous species.

SKI-BAR RANCH, 1940s. The Ski-Bar Ranch was open year-round, offering horseback riding during the summer and skiing throughout the rest of the year. When the road between Las Vegas and Mount Charleston was paved in the 1930s, many residents opted to spend their entire summers in the mountains.

GEORGE THOMPSON, 1939. The rapid increases in population brought a great deal of traffic to a town that had little preparation. The police department was kept very busy. In this photograph, George Thompson prepares for traffic detail on his motorcycle. Although a sergeant during the time of this photograph, Thompson was later appointed to chief of police.

Las Vegas Police Department, 1940. The small Las Vegas Police Department poses in front of two of its cars. With only a handful of officers in 1941, the Las Vegas Police Department responded to 127 cases of auto theft, 99 cases of drunk driving, and 1,390 accidents. Police Commissioner Pat Clark complained in 1943 that the driving public's "twin evils" were taxicab drivers and speeders.

Desert Love Buggy, Late 1930s. Made from a car kit ordered from the Sears catalog, the Desert Love Buggy was painted in brilliant colors and could be seen at many special events in Clark County. Here it is in front of the El Portal Theatre, alongside a ship, promoting the release of the film *Rulers of the Sea*.

Ambassador Motel, 1940s. A child stands on the running board of a car parked in front of the "air-cooled" Ambassador Motel at 1912 East Fremont Street.

Helldorado, 1935. In the 1930s, Las Vegas attracted tourists with promises of a frontier experience. This frontier spirit was celebrated in the annual "Helldorado Days." Hosted by the Elks Club, the town held a rodeo, a parade, and other festivities. Residents and tourists dressed in flashy Western-inspired clothing—those who did not, faced being "arrested." Seen here are residents in their Western finery during the first Helldorado. Helldorado was a community event. Six Companies, the contractor for the Hoover Dam project, provided transportation; grocery stores offered special sale items; casinos entered elaborate floats for the parade; and beauty salons created special hairdos for the event. Identified in this photograph are Patrick Gallaghar in the buckskin jacket, Louise Fleour on the burro, and John Cahlan kneeling.

HELLDORADO PARADE, 1940S. Horses in a Helldorado parade pass the Frontier Club on Fremont Street. After the completion of Hoover Dam, Las Vegas businesses began to notice a slow down. Helldorado events, however, enticed visitors to Clark County and helped boost the economy. Las Vegas advertised that it was "still a frontier town," and visitors enjoyed the Wild West atmosphere of Helldorado Days.

COSTUME CONTEST, 1935. Women line up on stage to display their frontier-inspired costumes during the first Helldorado celebration. In addition to dressing in costume, some men participated in the festivities by growing their beards in anticipation for the Helldorado Whisker Derby Contest.

Rotary Club, Late 1930s. Nearly everyone in town participated in Helldorado events. Helldorado drew the community closer by the creation of shared memories, but it also increased the exposure of Las Vegas on a national level. Members of the Las Vegas Rotary Club, founded in 1923, were longtime participants in the annual celebration and are seen in this photograph.

War Bond Drive, 1942. When the United States entered World War II in 1941, Clark County became very active on the home front. Schools, community organizations, and even casinos helped in the effort. In this photograph, the Gay Nineties Bar in the Last Frontier Casino holds a war bond drive.

USO Club, 1943. The USO, or the United Service Organization, is a national group that began prior to World War II. Volunteers and members work to boost troop morale through a variety of activities. In this photograph, Clark County women serve food to local soldiers. Journalist Florence Lee Jones Cahlan is seen third from left.

Las Vegas Gunnery School, 1942. When the army needed a location for weapons training, the expansive desert of Clark County was on the top of the list. The school opened in 1942. This photograph was taken during the first retreat ceremony (the end of the day and lowering of the flag) of the new installation.

Gunnery School Newspaper, 1943. A horned toad was the mascot for the gunnery school, and it was also the name of the school's newspaper. The school closed after the war but soon reopened as the Las Vegas Air Force Base in 1948. The base was renamed Nellis in 1950 in honor of Lt. William Nellis of Searchlight, who had been shot down and killed during the war.

GREY LADIES, 1942. Grey Ladies were Red Cross volunteers trained to work in hospitals. Since many nurses were needed to help with the armed forces, Grey Ladies were important in local hospitals. Seen here is the Clark County Grey Lady class of 1942, accompanied by two officers from the gunnery school.

IMPORTANT INSTRUCTIONS

1. Coupons can be used only in connection with the vehicle described on the front cover. Detached coupons are VOID.
2. If you stop using your car, this book and all unused coupons must be surrendered to your Board within 5 days.
3. If you sell your car, this book and all unused coupons must be surrendered to your Board. The purchaser will not be issued a gasoline ration unless he presents the receipt which you receive at the time of such surrender.

☆ GPO

FOLD HERE

A BASIC MILEAGE RATION

UNITED STATES OF AMERICA
OFFICE OF PRICE ADMINISTRATION

NAME OF REGISTERED OWNER John R. Dykstra

ADDRESS—NUMBER AND STREET

CITY AND STATE Las Vegas, Nevada

LICENSE No. AND STATE 17-786 Nev. | YEAR MODEL AND MAKE '28 Ford

Holder must fill in any blank spaces above before the first purchase of gasoline.

016687

OPA FORM R-525 C A17 MILEAGE 016687 (License No.) (State)

OPA FORM R-525 C A16 MILEAGE 016687 (License No.) (State)

MILEAGE RATION STAMPS, 1940S. The U.S. government instituted rationing during the war years in order to make sure that the country was able to meet the extraordinary supply needs of the armed forces. These ration stamps belonged to a Las Vegas resident.

BASIC MAGNESIUM, 1942. Magnesium, used in the construction of airplanes, became very important during the war. Under a contract with the U.S. government, Basic Magnesium, Inc. (BMI) began plans to construct a massive facility in the Clark County desert. The photograph above, taken in May 1942, marked the completion of the facility. BMI was a magnet for many looking for work. Thousands poured into Clark County in anticipation of working at the world's largest magnesium plant. Nearly 15,000 people moved to Clark County in hopes of working for BMI.

Basic Town Site, 1942. BMI provided homes for families as well as dorms for individuals, and like previous workers on the Hoover Dam, workers at BMI lived in tent cities while waiting for housing to be built. In this aerial view of the southern portion of the town site, the women's dormitory (center left) is still under construction. Basic later changed its name to Henderson, in honor of U.S. senator and Nevadan, Charles Henderson, who pushed for the construction of the magnesium plant.

Family in Carver Park, 1940s. Many of the workers who came to BMI were African Americans. The Williams family was the first to move into Carver Park, a segregated housing community for BMI employees. Even with the housing provided by BMI, there were not enough homes in Carver Park for African American workers, and many moved to the west side of Las Vegas.

St. Rose De Lima Hospital, Late 1940s. The hospital on East Lake Mead Drive in Henderson was originally named BMI Hospital and served workers from the plant. In 1947, the Adrian Dominican Sisters purchased the hospital for $1.

Frontier Radio, Late 1940s. Frontier Radio and Repair was located at 323 South Fifth Street in Las Vegas. As television gained popularity in the 1950s, the store added "television" to its name and began selling television sets along with its radios.

El Rancho Vegas, 1940s. In 1931, Nevada legalized gambling. Casinos became commonplace, but it wasn't until 10 years later that a casino was merged with a hotel to create an all-inclusive resort. El Rancho Vegas was the first major resort built on Highway 91, the road later named Las Vegas Boulevard. The most recognized image of Las Vegas shows the Las Vegas Strip, which is located in Clark County and is not governed by the city of Las Vegas.

FRONT OF EL RANCHO VEGAS, 1954. The El Rancho Vegas was created by Thomas Hull, who was inspired by the possibility of tourism generated by the Hoover Dam. Guests could relax at the health club or pool during the day and then enjoy an evening performance from stars like Sophie Tucker or Benny Goodman. The hotel's history was cut short when the main building was burned beyond repair in 1960. Although the hotel was small compared to those that are now on the Las Vegas Strip (it opened with just over 60 rooms), El Rancho Vegas set the precedent for the inclusive hotel-casino.

Hotel Last Frontier, 1940s. The Last Frontier opened shortly after its neighbor, El Rancho Vegas. In the picture above, the Little Church of the West is located on the right. The church is still in use as a wedding chapel but has been moved from its original location. Pictured below is the Ramona room, a combination dinner theater room and dance area. Owners invited guests to experience the "early west in modern splendor." The Hotel Last Frontier was inspired by images of the Old West, and the theme fit seamlessly into the town's Helldorado celebrations. The Frontier Village adjacent to the hotel featured historical artifacts collected from across the American West.

GLITTER GULCH, 1940S. The photograph at left was taken from the vantage point of a Shell gas station that was later replaced by the Fremont Hotel. The Golden Nugget was built in 1946 and is still open. This area of Fremont Street, seen below at night, is nicknamed Glitter Gulch for all of the brightly lit neon signs. In 1995, the area was closed to traffic and covered with a canopy of lights to create the Fremont Street Experience.

American Legion Auxiliary, 1947. The American Legion and its women's auxiliary first formed after World War I. Comprised of veterans, the American Legion works to advance the interests of veterans. Members have participated in war relief efforts for every American war. In this photograph are members of the Las Vegas women's auxiliary.

St. Joan of Arc Grotto, 1944. This grotto, dedicated to Our Lady of Lourdes, was designed and paid for by David Lorenzi in 1941. The grotto is part of the St. Joan of Arc Parish, established in Las Vegas in 1908. The church has been holding mass in the same building since 1939.

Downtown Buildings, 1940s. The combined post office and courthouse was built in 1933. Located at Third Street and Stewart Street, the building is now on the National Register of Historic Places and owned by the City of Las Vegas. When Las Vegas outgrew the mission-style depot built in 1905 (see page 10), it was replaced in 1940 with the structure below built in the streamline moderne style. This new rail station was built in the same location as the original depot but was torn down in the late 1960s to make way for the Union Plaza Hotel.

D-4-C Ranch, 1940s. In the early 1930s, Nevada changed its laws to make it easier to obtain a divorce. Many came to the state and stayed for at least six weeks to meet Nevada residency requirements. A new industry was born, and entrepreneurs created divorce ranches like the D-4-C ("divorcee"). Located in Clark County, outside of Las Vegas, the ranch was owned by cowboy actor Hoot Gibson. Below is a photograph of a helpful sign in the desert, pointing D-4-C visitors to Las Vegas.

Warehouse Fire, 1947. A fire began at the shared warehouse of the Las Vegas Distributing Company and the Utah Wholesale Grocery Company when transients built a fire under a loading dock to keep warm. It took an hour to control the fire, and three firemen suffered injuries.

Firemen's Ball Program, 1947. Hosted by the Firemen's Benefit Association, the Firemen's Ball began in 1947. The group's main purpose was to raise money to support firemen and their families when in need.

BLUE DIAMOND SCHOOL, 1942. This one-room schoolhouse was located in Blue Diamond, a ranching community to the west of Las Vegas. The students are unidentified, but to the left is Marion Werner, a visiting nurse from the Clark County Health Department.

WESTSIDE SCHOOL, 1940S. Westside Las Vegas, the original location of the McWilliams town site, was primarily an African American neighborhood because of segregation policies throughout town. The Westside School, however, was not segregated, and many groups attended it, including Native Americans. However, by the 1940s, it was a predominantly African American school. In this photograph, teacher Margaret Welch reads to her students.

HOOVER DAM AND LAKE MEAD, 1940S. After the war, Clark County turned to tourism as its main industry. Airlines promoted the many recreational features of Clark County, and many offered package deals at affordable prices. In this Transcontinental and Western Air publicity shot, three models appear to marvel at Hoover Dam, Lake Mead, and the surrounding desert. Billboards for casinos began appearing on highways as far away as Hollywood, and national celebrities like Bob Hope joined in Helldorado celebrations. Clark County's efforts at promoting itself were beginning to pay off.

Three

Communities and Casinos

Civil Defense, 1950s. W. Sholes and Ed Taylor of the Sheriff's Mounted Posse make plans during a training exercise with the Clark County Civil Defense. During the cold war, the civil defense conducted many such exercises with local groups in an attempt to prepare for any attacks or disasters. They were especially active in schools, where they taught students how to "duck and cover" and had a club for children interested in civil defense with a cartoon mascot named Burt the Transmuted Turtle.

Jeep Patrol, 1950s. The Jeep Patrol of the Clark County Civil Defense regularly drove through the desert, using detailed maps to aid their progress. During their missions, they sometimes staged mock rescues. They practiced desert survival skills and first aid.

Civil Defense ID Card, 1951. The Clark County Civil Defense was a large organization with several branches. The civil defense kept the public notified of nuclear tests in nearby Nye County. They also assisted the police when needed and helped supply fallout shelters. Members in Clark County had membership cards like the one shown here.

361 CIVIL DEFENSE IDENTIFICATION
CLARK COUNTY, NEVADA

CD

Auxiliary Police — 10-15-51
CIVIL DEFENSE ASSIGNMENT — DATE OF ISSUE

NORMAN C. NASH
ISSUED TO

915 MELROSE DRIVE LAS VEGAS
ADDRESS

SEX M AGE 42 WT. 160 HT. 5.11

HAIR LT BROWN EYES BLUE

IS A REGISTERED MEMBER OF THE CIVIL DEFENSE CORPS OF CLARK COUNTY, NEV.

Glen Jones
CHIEF OF DIVISION

L. B. Crandall
DIRECTOR

Norman C. Nash
SIGNATURE OF BEARER

Jets at Nellis, around 1950. Developed in the late 1940s, the T-33 aircraft shown here at Nellis Air Force Base were training jets with enough room in the cockpit for a pilot and instructor. Nellis, formerly the Las Vegas Gunnery School, is known as the "home of the fighter pilot." Pilots trained at Nellis played a crucial role in the Korean War.

THUNDERBIRDS, LATE 1950S. The Thunderbirds, the air force's flying demonstration team, was established at Luke Air Force Base in Arizona. The team was moved to Nellis Air Force Base in Clark County, Nevada, in 1956. It was at this time that the team began flying the F-100 Super Sabre fighter jets shown in this photograph.

Girl with Bow and Arrow, 1952. Marilee Knox poses with a bow and arrow outside her parents' home in the Huntridge Addition of Las Vegas. During the huge population jump in the 1940s, federal money was used to develop housing for people working in the war industries. The Huntridge Theatre, seen in the background, opened in 1944. It was a popular source of entertainment for locals and their families. Below, an ice cream truck stops on Norman Street in the Huntridge neighborhood.

El Tovar Auto Court, 1952. This auto court was located on 610 South Fremont Street near Bonneville Avenue. The word "motel" is a combination of "motor" and "hotel," and it is indicative of the American fascination with cars following World War II. As a way to entice drivers off the highway, most local motels and hotels had air-conditioning by the 1950s.

Boulder Dam Hotel, 1951. Built between 1933 and 1935, the Boulder Dam Hotel has hosted many famous celebrities, including Bette Davis, Will Rogers, and Boris Karloff. The Boulder City Hotel is still in operation and is home to the Boulder City/Hoover Dam Museum.

El Rey Club, 1950s. The El Rey Club was in Searchlight, a former mining town approximately 30 miles south of Boulder City. Before the club had access to a phone, owner Willie Martello is reported to have relayed messages to Las Vegas using carrier pigeons. Below, women pose for a publicity shot at the El Rey Club. In 1953, Martello's gaming license was revoked after he was accused of setting up a slot machine so that it would not pay out.

Willie Martello and Staff, 1952. Martello (left) and El Rey Club staff stand behind the polished bar with a wide array of guns. The El Rey Club was small, but it did have several table games in its casino. Although Martello denied it, the El Rey Club was rumored to be a brothel. In 1962, Martello sold the El Rey Club. Just days later, the club was almost completely destroyed by fire.

Willie Martello and Chef, 1952. The El Rey Club had a reputation in Clark County for good food. The expression on Willie Martello's face is proof. A writer in a 1964 issue of the *Nevadan* reminisced that the El Rey Club had "prime rib dinners not even a Californian could scoff at." Despite his questionable business practices, many Searchlight residents have fond memories of Martello allowing children to play in the El Rey Club swimming pool.

Mount Charleston Skiers, Undated. Skiers stand outside a snow-covered building at Mount Charleston. Tourist guides described the area as "the Switzerland of the desert." In the 1960s, Warren "Doc" Bailey, owner of the Hacienda Hotel, began investing in Mount Charleston properties. Already a resort area for locals, Mount Charleston began attracting out-of-towners.

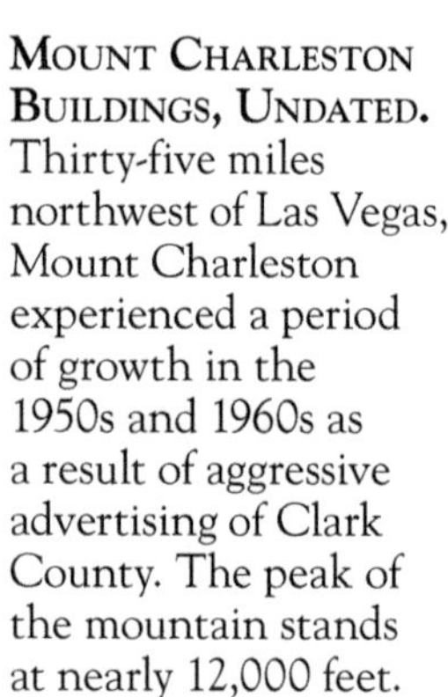

Mount Charleston Buildings, Undated. Thirty-five miles northwest of Las Vegas, Mount Charleston experienced a period of growth in the 1950s and 1960s as a result of aggressive advertising of Clark County. The peak of the mountain stands at nearly 12,000 feet.

Cold Creek, 1960s. In this photograph, a young boy, Richard "Tick" Segerblom, today a Nevada state assemblyman, is fishing at Cold Creek. Named for a creek in the Spring Mountains, Cold Creek is a small community in the Mount Charleston area. It is popular among local hikers as well as horse enthusiasts because of the area's large wild horse population.

Las Vegas Anniversary, 1955. On the 50th anniversary of Las Vegas, journalist Florence Lee Jones Cahlan wrote the entire issue and Bill Bailey managed all of the advertisements. In this photograph, they have spread the pages of the issue on the floor of a school gymnasium.

SNOW AT CAHLAN HOME, 1955. In January 1955, Las Vegas experienced its first snowstorm in six years. In this photograph, the home of Florence Lee Jones Cahlan and John Cahlan, writers for the *Review-Journal,* is covered in snow. Although Mount Charleston is covered in snow for much of the year, the valley areas of Clark County see it rarely and are therefore ill equipped. During this snowstorm, local flights were grounded, and Highland Park Elementary School was forced to close because of a broken furnace.

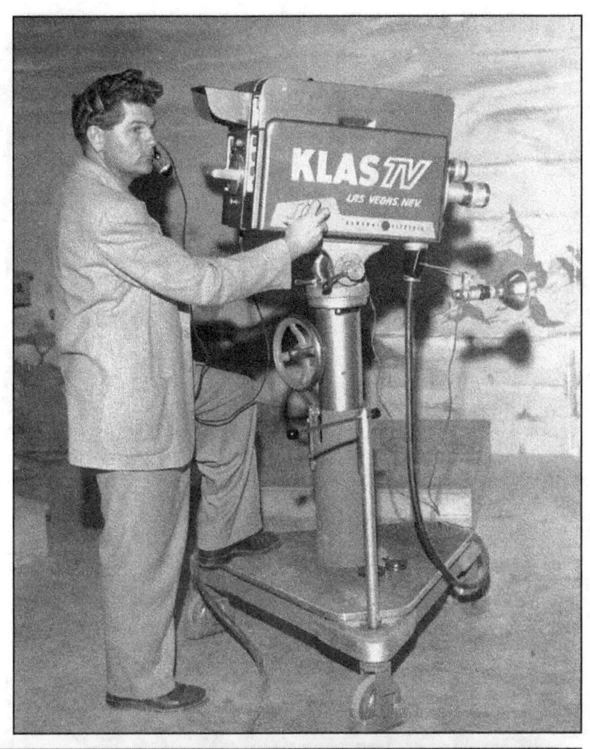

Media Outlets, 1950s. Cameraman Robert Allen stands by his camera at KLAS-TV. Founded by Hank Greenspun in 1953, KLAS was purchased by Howard Hughes in 1967. Hughes enjoyed being able to watch movies in private and grew annoyed when a late-night movie on KLAS was not to his liking. He purchased the station so he could control what was played. Longtime residents like to tell stories about the station suddenly switching to a different movie in response to the billionaire's request. In the photograph below, Jack Kogan and Anne Marie Preston are pictured during a broadcast of *Midnite Along Fremont Street* with Jack Kogan. Jack Kogan hosted late-night movies on television and had a series of radio shows, including interviews with many of the celebrities who performed in Las Vegas.

Las Vegas Parade, 1950s. The United Veterans of the Spanish-American War was a national group with a large branch in Las Vegas. Auxiliary membership was open to women who were relatives of the "Boys of 98," so-called because the Spanish-American War was fought in 1898. The veterans are seen here in a Las Vegas parade, perhaps Helldorado.

ATOM BOMB WATCHERS SOCIETY, 1951. When the Nevada Test Site began performing aboveground nuclear tests in nearby Nye County, Las Vegas journalists in charge of reporting on the tests formed the Atom Bomb Watchers Society. Here they are celebrating their first meeting with a rocket-shaped cake.

ONE-ARMED BANDITS, 1950S. Slot machines are nicknamed "one-armed bandits," and in this photograph, slot machines at the Las Vegas Club live up to their name.

SHOWGIRL, 1960S. This unidentified showgirl is representative of the glamour and beauty associated with classic Las Vegas shows.

Flamingo, 1954. Although Benjamin "Bugsy" Siegel has been portrayed as the creative force behind the Flamingo, Billy Wilkerson was the man who envisioned the casino. Siegel forced Wilkerson out of the project by the time it opened in 1946. Siegel was unable to make viable plans without the aid of Wilkerson and had to temporarily close the casino shortly after its awkward grand opening.

1956 THE Flamingo HOTEL
LAS VEGAS, NEVADA
THIS WILL INTRODUCE
KENNETH VanVORST
UPON PRESENTATION OF THIS CARD BEARING HIS SIGNATURE AND DULY COUNTERSIGNED IS ENTITLED TO CREDIT PRIVILEGES
BY Albert Parvin PRESIDENT
COUNTERSIGNED
Kenneth A. Van Vorst
SIGNATURE
No. CL 1051

Flamingo Credit Card, 1956. Casinos offered credit to preferred guests. This Flamingo credit card was issued to Las Vegan Ken Van Vorst.

Dunes Entrance, 1950s. The 85-acre resort, called the "Miracle in the Desert," was one of several hotel-casinos to adopt an Arab-inspired theme. Others included the Sands, Sahara, and the Aladdin. The fiberglass sheik guarding the entrance was 35 feet tall.

Dunes Sheik, 1950s. Kermit Wayne, a designer for the Young Electric Sign Company (YESCO), sketched this concept image of the Dunes Sheik. YESCO was responsible for creating a majority of the area's famous signage.

Dunes Opening, 1955. At the time of its completion, the Dunes was located on the southern reaches of the Las Vegas Strip. Over the years, expansion continued past the Dunes. The casino offered a variety of shows, a spa, and several restaurants.

Casino de Paris, 1960s. The Casino de Paris was one of many French revues featured in Las Vegas. Shows like Casino de Paris were key to developing the image of the classic Las Vegas showgirl, as seen on this Dunes envelope.

Downtown Las Vegas, 1950s. In this aerial photograph, Fremont Street is in the center. The rail station is in the bottom center.

Green Shack, Undated. Located at 2504 Fremont Street, the Green Shack restaurant was created by Mattie Jones in the early 1930s. The restaurant received much of its business from dam workers but remained a popular hangout even after the dam was completed. Bands like the one shown here began playing in the restaurant in the 1940s.

Station 2 Fire Truck, 1950s. Harold Knox, resident of the Huntridge neighborhood in Las Vegas, is at the wheel of the ladder truck. The Clark County Fire Department expanded in the 1940s and 1950s in response to the continual growth of residential areas.

Beta Sigma Phi, 1953. Sorority members of Beta Sigma Phi were active in the community and often held fashion shows to raise money for various charities. In this photograph, the president of the sorority, Pauline Barlow, is giving a VibraBath, a piece of hydrotherapy equipment, to the Easter Seals. In the center is Cathy O'Donnell, and on the left is Blanche Huffacker, director of the Easter Seals Treatment Center.

Gas Station, 1950s. This gas station was owned by "Pop" Simon and was located on the corner of Third and Fremont Streets. Although new hotels and casinos continued to open on Fremont Street, future development and tourists concentrated on the Las Vegas Strip in Clark County.

Entrance to Twin Lakes Lodge, 1950s. Formerly the Twin Lakes Resort, a dude ranch popular among divorcés, the newly named Twin Lakes Lodge offered many of the same diversions (see page 57). Visitors and locals could enjoy swimming, horseback riding, dancing, and rowboats. In 1950, a new housing development of over 600 homes was built near the Twin Lakes Lodge.

POOL AT TWIN LAKES, 1950S. The pool at Twin Lakes was popular with locals, especially during the summer. The Twin Lakes Lodge is now called Lorenzi Park and is owned by the City of Las Vegas. Many of the old structures are gone, including the pool and fountain in these photographs, but versions of the lakes and some buildings remain. The Nevada State Museum and Historical Society moved to the park in 1982.

FIRST AND FREMONT STREETS, 1952. A woman crosses First and Fremont Streets on a windy day. Behind her are the Las Vegas Pharmacy and a sign reminding Las Vegans to vote.

SERVICE LEAGUE, 1950S. In this photograph, women of the Service League, the forerunner to the Junior League, are seen visiting the El Rancho Vegas. The group was formed in 1946 to help meet the needs of the rapidly growing community. Women were often at the center of community improvements, and by the 1950s, women had formed hundreds of organizations throughout Clark County.

Moulin Rouge, 1955. Located on Bonanza Road in Westside Las Vegas, the Moulin Rouge was the town's first integrated casino-hotel. Although many casinos employed African Americans and headlined performers like Sammy Davis Jr., African Americans were not permitted to stay in any of the hotels. In the photograph below, Moulin Rouge Casino entertainment director Clarence Robinson (right) is seen preparing dancers for the hotel's grand opening. Although the Moulin Rouge was popular with locals, it lasted less than six months. Historical evidence suggests that the closing was due to poor management, but some believe the casino's closing was a result of plans to keep African Americans out of the casino industry.

THEODORA "DOLCINIA" BOYD, 1955. Theodora Boyd, a Moulin Rouge showgirl, shows off at the swimming pool. In addition to a swimming pool, the Moulin Rouge had two full-service restaurants. Showgirls arrived from all over the United States to perform at the Moulin Rouge. In 1955, a photograph of the showgirls during their cancan dance made the cover of *Life* magazine. Moulin Rouge ran three shows a night, as opposed to the two normally found in casinos. The third show, which began at 2:00 a.m., was the most popular and attracted many celebrities.

Moulin Rouge Security Guards, 1955. The Moulin Rouge had an integrated clientele and staff. The Moulin Rouge was named after a club with the same name in Paris. Las Vegas hotels did not integrate until local civil rights leaders doctors James McMillan and Charles West threatened a highly publicized march on the Las Vegas Strip. Worried about the reaction of tourists, most casinos relented.

Thunderbird, 1954. The Thunderbird Hotel was built in 1948 across from the El Rancho Vegas on Highway 91, or the Las Vegas Strip. Instead of the grand casinos that were becoming popular in Las Vegas, the Thunderbird was designed to be more sedate and comfortable while maintaining high quality.

Turquoise Room, 1958. Although the Thunderbird was named and decorated according to popular images of Native Americans, this menu from the Turquoise Room featured French-inspired foods. The Thunderbird quickly gained national notoriety during the 1950 Kefauver trials, when the hotel's links to the mob were exposed. Its gaming license was suspended after owners received money from the brother of known gangster Meyer Lansky.

SOUTH PACIFIC, 1962. The Thunderbird became a hotspot for entertainment. In the 1960s, the hotel began running Rodgers and Hammerstein musicals, including *Flower Drum Song* and *South Pacific*. Despite the musicals, the Thunderbird could not compete with the bigger Las Vegas Strip casinos. Owners changed the name to the Silverbird and later El Rancho in honor of the strip's major resort. The hotel closed in 1992 and was later demolished.

LANDMARK HOTEL, 1960S. Frank Carroll began building the Landmark Hotel in 1960, but because of funding problems, the hotel didn't open until after Howard Hughes purchased the property in 1968. The hotel was located on Paradise Road, and its observation deck complemented the futuristic look of the nearby convention center. The hotel 1995 implosion was featured in the movie *Mars Attacks!* (1996).

Las Vegas Convention Center, 1960s. Built in 1959, the design of the convention center was reminiscent of a flying saucer, although the *Reno Evening Gazette* said the silver-colored aluminum dome was a nod to the Silver State. The spaceship effect was even more dramatic at night when the building was lit from below. At maximum capacity, the Convention Center could hold up to 18,000 people. It also became the home of the Convention Bureau and the Las Vegas News Bureau.

World Congress of Flight, 1959. The Las Vegas Convention Center opened in the spring of 1959. The first convention held in the new facility was the World Congress of Flight, seen here. The center was created as part of a plan to diversify the economy of Las Vegas.

Grocery Store Display, 1950s. An unidentified clerk stands next to a Canada Dry display. To the right of the display are jars of baby food.

American Linen, 1950s–1960s. Women sort laundry at the American Linen Supply Company. The store was located on 1001 First Street and was a large-scale operation with pick-up and delivery service.

Elevated View of Indian Springs, 1960s. Indian Springs, named for the artesian wells in the area, is located approximately 35 miles northwest of Las Vegas.

Water at Indian Springs, 1960s. A pool of water surrounded by trees is seen in this photograph in the town of Indian Springs.

Home at Indian Springs, 1960s. In the 1940s, Indian Springs became home to the Air Force Auxiliary Base. The base name was later changed to Creech Air Force Base.

Indian Springs, 1960s. Indian Springs was originally owned by a Native American named Old Ben. It became the MacFarland Ranch in the 1910s.

Pioneer Club Sign, Early 1950s. "Vegas Vic" points the way to Fremont Street's Pioneer Club. The Pioneer Club opened in 1942 and was topped by the full-size Vegas Vic in the early 1950s. The character has long been a symbol of Las Vegas. The Pioneer Club closed in the 1990s, but the image of Vegas Vic is still in Glitter Gulch.

Hacienda Pool, 1956. When the Hacienda Hotel opened in 1956, its Olympic-size swimming pool was reported to be the largest in Nevada.

The Boulder Club and Binion's Horseshoe, 1956. Locals Phyllis and Harold Knox pose in front of the Horseshoe's famous $1 million display. The Boulder Club was one of the earliest casinos in town but eventually fell out of favor once casinos began marketing themselves as resorts. The Boulder Club never fully recovered from a fire in the 1950s. The adjacent Binion's Horseshoe bought the older building so the newer casino could expand. In the photograph below, walls of the Boulder Club are torn down in preparation for its new owner in 1960.

CIRCUS CIRCUS, 1968. Designed to resemble a big-top tent, Circus Circus cost $15 million to build. Conceived by Jay Sarno, the same man who created Caesars Palace, Circus Circus was designed to be festive yet extravagant.

NEVADA CLUB, 1958. A family poses inside the Nevada Club, across the street from the Mint. The Nevada Club opened June 30th, 1954.

The Mint, 1961. Shown before the 1965 construction of its tower, the Mint was absorbed by Binion's Horseshoe in the 1980s. The Mint became famous for the Mint 400, an annual car race through the desert of Clark County. Author Hunter S. Thompson immortalized the race in his novel *Fear and Loathing in Las Vegas.*

Desert Inn, 1950s. Wilbur Clark's Desert Inn opened in 1950. Headliners like Frank Sinatra, Carmen Miranda, and Buddy Hackett were frequent performers at the resort casino. In this photograph, Ed Sullivan is listed on the marquee.

Aerial of Las Vegas, 1950s. In this aerial photograph, Fifth Street is at center and Charleston Boulevard is to the right.

Caesars Palace Swimming Pool, 1960s. Everything at Caesars Palace was built on a grand scale, including the swimming pool. At the time of its construction in 1966, Caesars was the biggest hotel on the Las Vegas Strip.

Caesars Palace Bacchanal Room, 1960s. Although inspired by ideas of Roman luxury, Caesars Palace was accessible to the average person. The Bacchanal Room was designed to make guests feel like kings—or Caesars. Guests could choose to be served by women dressed as goddesses.

NELSON'S LANDING, 1950S. Located in the Eldorado Canyon area, 25 miles south of Boulder City, Nelson's Landing was a significant supply port during the 19th century. No longer a port in the 1950s, it was a good place for catching trout, as the men are doing here.

ORAN GRAGSON AND SHRINERS, 1960S. Elected mayor of Las Vegas in 1959, Oran Gragson meets with members of the Al Kadosh Shrine. Part of the Masons, Shriners have contributed to their communities by helping provide health care for children with birth defects.

POST OFFICE BUILDING, 1967. This brochure is from the opening of the new main post office building built in 1967. It was located on 1001 Keno Lane (now Circus Circus Drive) by Industrial Road. The old downtown post office building was still used but with limited service.

COURTHOUSE, 1960S. Built in 1960, this courthouse was on Third Street and Carson Street in Las Vegas. While looking at the architectural drawings, District Judge George Marshall complained that the design was impractical. After the building was completed, however, employees found it suitable.

Sheriff's Mounted Posse, 1960s. The Sheriff's Mounted Posse was an all-volunteer group that began in 1947. They worked with local authorities to assist in search and rescue operations and participated in many community events.

Union Pacific Park, 1960s. Students of Cliff Segerblom practice painting in the picturesque Union Pacific Park in downtown Las Vegas. In addition to being a painter and teacher, Segerblom was a photographer and responsible for this image of his class.

Wagons and Burro Teams, 1966. On the 50th anniversary of the National Park Service, a wagon labeled "Cowboy Park or Bust" rolls through the intersection of Rainbow Boulevard and Charleston Boulevard. Although the area was desolate in the 1960s, it is now one of the busiest intersections in Las Vegas.

MAN AT ARROW CANYON, 1973. An unidentified man, photographed by Cliff Segerblom on an archaeological expedition in Arrow Canyon, is surrounded by Clark County desert. Arrow Canyon is 35 miles north of Las Vegas and is a federal wilderness area monitored by the Bureau of Land Management.

BIBLIOGRAPHY

Carlson, Helen S. *Nevada Place Names: A Geographical Dictionary*. Reno, NV: University of Nevada Press, 1974.

Land, Barbara, and Myrick Land. *A Short History of Las Vegas*. Reno, NV: University of Nevada Press, 1999.

Moehring, Eugene, and Michael Greene. *Las Vegas: A Centennial History*. Reno, NV: University of Nevada Press, 2005.

Paher, Stanley. *Las Vegas: As it Began—As it Grew*. Las Vegas, NV: Nevada Publications, 1971.

Wright, Frank. *Clark County: The Changing Face of Southern Nevada*. Las Vegas, NV: Nevada State Museum and Historical Society, 1981.

———. *Nevada Yesterdays*. Las Vegas, NV: Stephens Press, 2005.

www.ingramcontent.com/pod-product-compliance
Lightning Source LLC
LaVergne TN
LVHW081534100826
845153LV00004B/268

9781531645632